ISBN: 978-81-939295-3-7
First Edition: Feb 14, 2019
Cover Design: Akansha Kukreja
Funded by: *RædLeaf Foundation for Poetry & Allied Arts*
as a part of RL Poetry Awards winning series.

Poems
by

PREETI VANGANI

Winner
RL POETRY AWARD 2017
National (India) Category

For my mother

1962 - 2008

CONTENTS

II. Apologize

INTRODUCTION

"Poems are useless," begins the prose poem, "unless they are pepper spray, stinging cries for change, girls dancing fearless at night. I want poems my mother couldn't write in her book of recipes." Preeti Vangani is, as she freely admits, riffing on the African-American poet Amiri Baraka, who once claimed that poems were useless unless they could shoot, or provide us with daggers, or serve as our fists. Pepper spray and cries for change are more humane than fists and daggers, but Vangani's urgency is no less intense than Baraka's. Her poems constantly circle back to the condition of women, both in India and the world, and call for change. She honors her mother, whose struggles with cancer she documents in a number of her poems, but she yearns for a world larger than that which her mother was not permitted to inhabit. Her yearning takes the form of meditations on love and sex, on violence, fear, joy, and death. They are poems of feminist struggle— emphatically so. But it is because, not in spite, of this that they speak so directly and so powerfully to not only to women, and not only to Indians, but to that which is most human in all of us.

Vangani's work is formally various, even adventurous. Coming to poetry later in life than some, she approaches it with the zeal of a convert, looking for miracles in any form they take. Prose poems, list poems, poems using patterns of anaphora and verbal repetition, concrete poems, poems with footnotes, poems with missing words (sometimes silence speaks loudest of all), question & answer poems, poems both terse and voluble, confessional poems, erotic poems, elegiac poems, a poem in the form of a clock, a poem in the form of an instruction manual—there is nothing that her omnivorous imagination does not embrace, nothing from which her inventive muse shies away. Yet we always feel the presence of a voice addressing us: this is less poetry we overhear than it is poetry seeking us out and taking us aside. In this respect Vangani's roots in performance poetry make themselves present, though she has come a long way from being, as she once put it, "the person who carried a thick folder of poems at open mics in Bombay in hope that they'd let me read."

In the combination of political edge, formal adventurousness, and the energies of the performer's voice, Vangani strikes this American reader as similar to Airea D. Matthews, a recent winner of the prestigious Yale Series of Younger Poet's Prize. Perhaps the parallels between the Yale and RL Poetry Award winners indicate we're in for a worldwide renaissance of poets like Matthews and Vangani, poets who bring together energies most often found in isolation. Let's hope that will be the case, and take the publication of *Mother Tongue Apologize* as evidence that it can be so.

ROBERT ARCHAEMBEAU
Judge, RL Poetry Award 2017

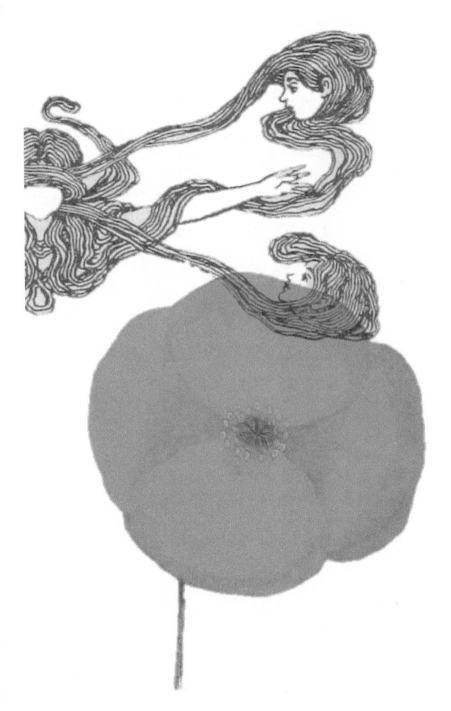

Unremember

One way of bringing you back is to observe
your garlanded frame as art: dying, obsolete
unappreciated between origami and handmade candles.
Another is to bring back the heat of imitation
leather from hospital guest beds. Who knew waiting rooms
were carriers of sweaty fevers, making it impossible to sieve
dream from memory: *What could I have said to raise you
from the dead?* What do volumes of elegies contain that I don't?
Their own inabilities to say the unsaid to the one who will
unsee unhear untouch unmove un-understand, understand
I am trying to backpack through the geography of a future
without you, my compass, and no one has written a Lonely
Planet Guide titled 100 Getaways Without Mother, or
let's produce a reality TV show for contestants to adventure
through losses on a shoestring budget: Today you are
not allowed to take the deceased's name. Today you are
not to remember the way she smiled when she said yours.
You cannot hold faith as a torch light over reality's head.
You will be disqualified if you re-enter the symmetry
of this world with longing as your wild card. For your last
challenge, you must dump the vanishing remains into a glass
exhibit and create an event of everything that is, label it *was.*

I.

Mother Tongue

ABCs of Hostel Sex

At 22, still untouched, I opened my legs to another
blood: a collateral; girls shed easy. Convinced myself
Consider the respect if you did 'it'? So I did 'it' and later
danced into the verandah, announced my
excitement buttoned up in the boy's shirt.
F word an F word, I whispered the F word but not as a curse
(girl's got game, my roommate said, and she's got
hickeys the size of acid bug bites).
I remember mid-'it', moaning *You can come inside.* Outside
just a June noon, some rowdies playing Counterstrike.
Kissed goodbye to saving it for my husband.
Licking my boyfriend's ear, I felt him pulse, it must be dark
magic, *you are my number*
nine, he spilled while spooning.
One was his 'dirty' married neighbor, he boasted
pointing to the Kleenex box.
Quickly, how swiftly he could unhook clasps.
Right there, keep going, a little lower
so good, you feel so good he whispered:
Turn please quick and beyond the headboard I saw my
unscrupulous
virginity bunched up in old jeans on the floor of a 9x5 room
with care packages from home. Popping out of a transparent folder,
Xeroxes of identity cards, and my dad's warning:
you must keep these in a safe place, always
zipped up.

I
AM
MOA
NING
AT YOUR
KINDNES
SENDING BE
TWEEN MY LEGS

Stopgap

I opened another hole in my body
so you could take more pleasure
in untouched parts of me.
(Sometimes) your touch was in your gaze.

So you may take more pleasure
I pierced my bellybutton this time.
Your touch was in your gaze:
unsure, loose, shifty.

The time I pierced my bellybutton
you called me sexy, hot, cheap,
unsure, loose, shifty.
You wanted me turned around sometimes.

You called me sexy, hot, cheap
when I imitated the item-song girl's pelvic thrust
you wanted me turned around. Sometimes,
your eyes closed, you imagined her instead,

you saw me imitate the item-song girl's pelvic thrust
and said: *Too vulgar, I don't want my girl to do this.*
Your eyes closed, you imagined her instead
stroking a side of you, you don't let me touch.

Say, isn't it too vulgar for a girl to do this:
Sucking tight at the edges of holes,
stroking every side of you. Yet you don't let me
touch the seams of an everyday kind of love.

Sucking tight at the edges of holes –

my body is a sieve that continues to hold
nothing. In untouched parts of me
I opened another hole in my body.

Visiting Hours

The evening
it came to light
Ma had cancer,
in three parts
Pa broke his fistula.
Together in sickness.

Their blood trails
everywhere like bread crumbs:
I follow them home.

Genealogy

My body is a collage made with all my little toes, swollen
and rough like ginger. I come from my mother's mother:
last seen falling off the edge of our balcony, or did she jump?
How everything changes when a door is gone, some conjure
Alzheimer's, some depression and to my date I say, I come
from a family of uncorseted women. I keep on running
into the alleyways of my arthritic folds and whisper
to the unnatural bends of my elbows and knuckles.
When I was one, I was unscathed by a fall, the thud of my skull,
against our floral tile breaking my grandma's nap. In the hospital
she shook my head, thrice yes, thrice no to force a cry. I hide
myself in the clench of my jaw and talk about my pain: a moving
target, the bureau's forecast about yesterday – overcalled, off,
formulaic. I curl tight in my fist all the versions of what I could be:
a history teacher, a saree folder, the sizzle of jeera
in ghee, the ruffle of pashmina sliding through a finger ring,
the inside of my mother's palm. I fall often like the unsure wind
falls over a teenage girl's petal tally of loves/loves me not.
I hanker for the whiff of love like sweet and spicy rough cuts
of mango pickle lingering on my tongue, swallowed whole,
each of my loves a raw fruit amply marinated in a May sun,
preserved on a forgotten shelf. I want to crush strawberries
in the face of the man who once filled me
with cynicism. I sleep well only in motion and wake up on buses
once my home is a blur over my shoulder. I slumber in a city
built by flyovers, dying under its own weight. On the blues I fall
like a torrential downpour, until you wonder who's the real boss in the
metropolitan of my heart. I am in the fingerprints on the butter tray
licked clean when ma was asleep. I think myself a realistic Krishna,
a compulsive flirt masquerading as god, singing songs when logic fails
reason fails fate fails prayer fails my mother's prayer beads.

In her room, by the window there was an ironing table,
hot steam straightening weary shirt collars. Between the creases
of five languages known to me, I learnt to swear from my father.
The only daughter of his name. My name is Sanskrit
for pleasure, joy, love: all the bloody words
a poem should never engrave.

Saat Samundar Paar Main Tere Peeche Peeche Aa Gayi

Song title: I crossed seven oceans to come see you

in the year of no jeans fitting me right
i sit in the shape of a tear,
face stuck to the shut white door

my favorite song which has three actresses dancing
plays inside, two cousin sisters dancing on the round spring bed
have locked me out, despite me rehearsing all the steps

swing tap swing bang arms and feet, i repeat
my routine for the door
i will be happy with the back row too

(years later the lead actress, Divya Bharti
will have jumped from her balcony
and we will miss her in the songs to come)

i can hear them pressing rewind
on the tape recorder, and then pause
going back and forth, will they let me in?

i wail and beg as i attempt getting up
from the deep end of my pool of tears
i could have been the missing actress

i am thirteen and a half years old

and the only friends that don't stop talking to me
are the pimples on my face

no other cousin must use Eskinol Pimple Fight
from Dubai, which burns the skin; mummy swears
that acne will go if I stop thinking

no boy talks to me in coaching class
i have all the answers and i'm OK
with them copying from my answer sheet

why can't I transform into grandma's age instantly?
Amma has clear skin, a husband,
no cousins lock doors on her

what they do without me
i feel behind closed doors,
the keyhole is on my side

they criticize that I talk too loudly
but I am not sure my banging voice
reaches them at all

Shorthand: Violence

a) Physical Force
Any minute the curl of his fingers
caressing a scotch glass
can round into a fist crashing//\\the spine of a wall
my father   his love
a complex blend
held in oak with finishing notes
                              of honey

b) Self-directed
look up 'how to kill' >> refuse to look up >> at ceiling fan
look up at the insects >> on the night lamp >> verify if dead
or wise with too much light

c) Threatened or actual
All letters are odes to spaces
mother left behind. Addressed to father
never to be sent

d) Intentional Use
The year I forgot to notice your refusals of sex
each time I was the one asking. Your hunger
must be served, not induced

e) Deprivation
All of the above

Waterlogging

I think about the mornings it saved me
to see children splatter the Bombay monsoons
with paper boats. Their miniature palms folding

into their mothers', two sizes too big, their raincoats
with dewy edges, hanging at the mercy of pastel plastic
clips. Zigzagging through a row of chipped roof huts

the wiper of my second-hand purple car, outstretched,
groaning its rubbery groan to drive away water from my view.
The road ahead: cloud-gray, washed out, slipping into its own

bends; like a body being reborn when it lets itself break
down in full public view. Each hawker and beggar negotiating
their wishes under the tick-tock of limited dry hours. This city,

flooding. My heart like this city, a closed island with eighteen
million impulses stirring, pumping in and out of crevices, to find refuge
under the radii of tin shelters or the hemline of an umbrella.

Inside, a water cooler sweating itself in the waiting
room, the slow drip of glucose reaching mother's veins, my hand
turning another blotted page, as Kundera says, *love is the longing*

for the half of ourselves we have lost. One abandoned shoe
floating in the slight rainbows of puddles. The doctor shaking
his pen as he talks about options. Does the sky know of all it lets go

and all it holds back, and does my memory? Walking through it all
waist deep, students wading with backpacks over their heads,
every lane & by-lane, a canopy of escape routes. A 12-inch

flat screen TV being banged from the side. Intermittent cable service and flashes of a news anchor lady asking the weatherman for a statistic on the level of water harvested thus far.

House Red

In her cream laced handkerchief mother is vomiting
blood like clouds I make shapes in anything she discards
these days my heart is blotting like disordered ink
of a Rorschach test appropriately deranged I see a knight falling
see a butterfly crushed by a bootheel in her dry eyes
I see blackberries rotting & blood lines her manicured nails
wrinkled wrists at best a nest for needles too thin for a bangle she filled
out plump like a wineglass' bowl reduced to stem what can one hold
on to when one has lost half of all their blood

What of Love?
No, What of It Really?

My mom makes breakfast, lunch, and dinner
My father goes to his saree shop
My mom deals with my exam atrocities
My father asks *Will you come first this time in class again?*
My mom turns prayer beads 1188 times for an easy question paper
My father goes to the shop
My mom makes a feast at the drop of a guest
My father brings me firecrackers
My mom cries and whimpers
My father raises his voice, my mom does too
I cry
My father asks *Have you learnt this crying drama from your mom?*
We don't have a carpet in our house but oh if we did
Sweep sweep sweep, everything goes under
My mom is married to a kitchen
My father to his shop
I learn up the words to the latest love song
This is what I know of love, mostly

Ma Sang Ghazals as She Oiled My Hair

To find bits of you in the mirror, I let down my hair
I've got Pa's jaw and nose, but you stay wound in my hair.

A cup of hot Horlicks shakes in my hands as you plait
my alopecia. Baldness braids a frown in my hair.

Golden Globes on TV, Sarandon crossing fingers
in a red gown, for Stepmom. She loses by a hair.

Jagjit Singh on the radio, as you massage my scalp,
your fingers dance to his ghazal sounds in my hair.

Eggs, beer, Shikakai, henna. Each Sunday afternoon
we tried a new magic potion to turnaround our hair.

To make lung cancer lighter, I got you a headscarf
with marijuana leaves, joking weed will grow where hair

cannot; a day pass without you falling in the grey
of my carpet & pillowcase -- resting grounds of this hair.

I want to lean on you like the curl resting on your shoulder,
your absence is a dark number equal to strands found in this hair.

"Chikoo," you'd warn "don't laugh at my off-key singing
...you'll remember it abound once I'm out of your hair".

Science of Loss

I saw my mother for a total of three times over the
two years that she lived with that thing in her left
breast which came back in her lung. I couldn't gather
words in my mouth when someone asked, I'd say Not
Serious, Getting Better, Doctor Unsure but never
cancer. I saw her gathering her hair to one side:
straight brown silk falling when she combed it to
cover as much baldness as she could. I saw locks
falling in the feet of the little temple that lies below a
full-length mirror in her room. She held them the way
she held a lost sparrow that once found its way into
our balcony. Hair is anyway dead, isn't it? She folded
her palms in prayer, as if making an offering of hair, I
wonder what she asked for that afternoon. Did she ask
for her illness to recede, for her hair to be reborn? But
knowing her I was certain she just said let nothing like
that ever happen to her daughter. *May my daughter's hair
grow long, longer than me, may she live longer than me.* After
she left us, I opened her progress files. Scans, MRIs,
X-rays exposing life-taking tumors on a life-giving
body. I read each binder, decoding its science,
dropping of blood corpuscles, prescriptions of pills,
anta-acids and anti-depressants. Rate of radiation,
catharsis of chemotherapy, dosage of drugs, diaries of
deterioration. I learnt and spoke cancer in hope that
she'd be back because I had acknowledged her
suffering and its name. I have taken this science, made
it my own, every time I cough I run to WebMD and
key in my symptoms: a rash, a scratch, a sudden mole.
I absorb more science to learn about new diseases that
could connect me to her. I touch my body like the

health magazine says. Scan for lumps and swellings. But all I have is a swollen heart; no blood test can diagnose. The science of loss is lost in me.

Voice Over

Ma lived all her years in a before cell-phone era (B.C).
In her AD, I rechristened our landline from Home to Mummy
calling the number as one calls a fortune teller, peering
into the intricacies of crystal – my tears, globes

floating on the receiver. I felt like all the mourners speaking to the *wind*
telephone – a phone booth in Japan, connected to nowhere,
built to air out grief. Being inside that space was the closest
I could get to floating

inside my mother, kicking around for answers, trying to satiate
a hunger I don't have a name for, wondering if waves can carry
what words cannot, if words are common city birds
slamming their wings against glass panes, mid-flight floating

this poem: part ruin part construction site, rumble on the other
side; I, my mouth open, encrypting the absent voice into a voice.

Joint Words

When I see infants being massaged in commercials
with fragrant baby oil, I get up from my cross-legged seat
and wince without showing. I got arthritis when I was 21.
It was my left ankle first – misdiagnosed as a hairline fracture.
From one ankle to the next, arthritis is more symmetrically
perfect than Angelina Jolie's face. The more I stay still,
the more it begins to hurt.

This body learns to survive, just as it learns to hide.
When my fingers give up, my elbows jump in
to open intimidating glass doors. I am slowly losing grip
on ears of mugs. My palms have no choice
but to befriend hot surfaces.

Despite physiotherapy and allopathy,
despite naturopathy and homeopathy,
my inflamed elbows get stuck when I want to hug you,
my stiff shoulder cracks each time you waltz with me.
In a drunken swirl, you bend me over
asking me to be more malleable and
I try.

There was nobody else at the time
dialoguing with my body as you were, yet
you chose to leave because this – this disease you said
was a liability for you.

I wanted to punch you that evening, but my hand couldn't
make a full fist.
This isn't a disease. It is an auto-
immune disorder. An abnormal immune response

where my body starts raising its temperature
even when nothing's wrong with it. I am the attacker
and the attacked.

I lace my swollen toes under closed shoes, find
reasons not to shake hands, pose in photographs
with my swan-neck deformities buried in pockets or shame.
These 10 fingers were once the object of pride
of a twelve-year-old Bharatnatyam dancer.
 Once, I was an expert at releasing
dancing-peacocks with my hands.

My hands are getting tired now but I will continue
to write. I will write until every single movement
that a healthy body performs is imagined fully
by my words. Until I have found new forms to crack open
window latches and tin cans, hold bus handles and hand brakes.
I will write because you, my deformities, need to make jagged
handprints –
again and again until this becomes an acceptable mould.

Visiting Hours

Soot covered poster

hangs in Oncology:

Is your Love Insured

Second Guessing

As we see the nurse lifting ma's comatose head to change her pillow
my brother asks if I will ever write about this and I say – nothing
to write about when I want to be able to say there's nothing

to worry about. Her eyes will open any second and carry off our worries
like a file of ants marching with a grain of sugar. She will be back
to being an army that searches, collects, sustains for the cold future.

The last time she was conscious she asked for her sister
who thinks Ma's silence got clogged in her breast like hair in the drain.
Another aunt says ma drank too much tea. Papa's fingers are tapping

ma's lung x-rays and a rich cousin is certain that Papa skimped on the
class of hospitals. Send her to London she states, rates of survival are
better in the west. Tie a black thread around

her ankle, says grandma, positive that a raw egg circled over a sick body
is enough to drive bad spirits away. As we see the nurse fluffing
her pillow, all I want is to be able to write

myself into the hallways of my mother's dreams. Put my good writing
hand where her pillow is and second guess: How far into her sleep
did she reverse her belief in god? Instead in this room that diagnoses

and breeds a healthy dose of loss, I re-rehearse all the signs I know
for a college charades contest. A *name* is a pat on the heart. A *family*
is holding one's hands out and folding palms as if forming a human
fence.

At the ICU I Think of Wall of Death:

a sideshow at a carnival
        a motorcyclist horizontal, on a vertical wall

intersecting the edges every night, a spectacle
        some visitors think is an amusement; uncertain

if their children should witness
        my mother in her hospital bed losing

memory, vision, & weight like a feather
        in motion, a rider circling on a machine

The on-looker like the head of a coin
        tossed in air erring too heavily

on one side of life: how many trips left
        around the same loop, how long until

questions with no mouths hang like creaking plastic
        chairs shifting forever to get better

views: snapping, cheering, clapping, anything
        to get hope's attention through a rusting fence

can you see, my second heart trapped in a giant cylinder
        and fate's eyes a convex rink opening closing opening

Last Rites

The aunt who yelled at ma when I was nine
is putting on redemption as make-up today, reciting
the Gita over ma's corpse: *Abandon all attachment*
to the results of action. An uncle makes phone calls
for mid-priced wood, says, *nothing too fancy.* I imagine
when he goes we'll scorch him on a pyre of cash bundles
that he's hoping to save off my mother's cold body.
She is now being rubbed in ghee for uniform burning. Look

at the neighbors looking down at you from windows
like your future is a video clip buffering. Ask the bodiless
sky for two more hands to juggle the *why m*e and *why her.*
In my mother's hometown, the word goodbye
is considered bad luck. Instead they leave their house
to *Aaujo: Come again.* Ask ma if she wants a pair
of housekeys just in case. The theatre of loss
has too many emergency exits. Push again to check
if any of those doors open the other way.

Repair & Maintenance

My father euphemizes going to poop as Vacation. An average trip
inside is thirty-five minutes *like a nice spa for my body*
he says, unless his phone rings inside & it is an aunt's son's
friend's uncle's cousin inquiring about the what, why, where, how,
what now of a certain cancer & through the bathroom door
I can hear him croon addresses of hospitals rehearsed, doctors
memorized by first names & specializations & a chorus
of home remedies as if treating cancer is his long-forgotten hobby.

Come stay with us, we'll fix together he says; this body trapped
in your mouth, chest, lung, stomach, colon. Then pauses & paces
in a retreat of his own inadequacies trying to redeem what he lost.
As if a stranger's life lengthened is my mother
reincarnated, as if becoming a bed & breakfast for cancer
is injecting grief with morphine, as if opening our doors
to another's suffering is my father testing his voice like a tourist
at the edge of Echo Point whispering *I tried I tried I tried.*

Mother's Day 2016

I rearrange the bangles on my left wrist, wonder if this is the day
we must replace ma's headshot from the imitation-gold family tree frame.
The entrance to the Gurudwara pools with moss, muck and guests
tiptoeing around the awkwardness of residual raindrops

falling like windfall losses from god's roof. Side hugs and flying kisses
are being passed around to bless the new couple, except one aunt
who rips the religious silence apart. She says to me sotto voce
Congratulations on your new mom you must be so happy.

I tuck myself into a corner with my phone as my father calls
his young wife's name aloud; Mamta - meaning a mother's love.
I stare deep into the walls of Facebook, plastered
with Mother's Day tributes, every stranger pretending

to be my friend here, asking me to comment. As I stand
in for a photo, something black and lumpy grows
between my ribs. It doesn't show when I say cheese; I hold my smile
like a clear ice cube resting on my bare skin for a very long time.

Admission

After Matthew Siegel

Within the sooty pages of a half-read memoir, I find a picture
of Papa and me. Taken after we tumbled out of the death-
defying rollercoaster ride. Hung lopsided, his smile -
unsure if he lost something when we were suspended
in glass capsules: his tooth filling, a pill, his hat or a little
of his head. I show him the picture, he laughs and brags
From when I had hair in a tenor with which a man remembers
the day he started trusting his wife. He asks me why
I don't smile with both dimples, outside of photos
I say *It was just a phase* when I want to say, *I just don't
get amused as easily.* As if in trade; he texts me a picture
of water chestnuts from a grocery aisle, captioned
Do you still love these? And I cry because I'm certain that
after he's gone, this question will follow me around
the way memory chases everything that slips away
between the gap in its teeth. It has taken me nine years
and ten months to let him into my silences – grief tucked within folds
of monosyllables: yes, no, hmmm.
I am leaning on him in the picture, shaking
a green soda can. A click, and we were both soaked
in an overflow of sugar and laughter. Now he sleeps alone on her side
of the bed. I tiptoe around the drapes, careful not to make
the curtain rings chime. He calls me *Pooja* meaning prayer –
my late mother's name, as he opens his eyes. I let the sun in
blind by blind. Wait until we adjust to the sudden light.

Mother's Legacy

+ Ash in newspaper packets
+ Bob cut wig of horse hair
+ *Om Namo Sai Allah Malik*, say it 1188 times
+ Emergency contact list in vanity box
+ Food is Medicine Vol. 8.1
+ Four cotton kurtas
+ Glass Lakshmi, goddess of wealth
+ Six eggs, tomatoes 1kg, dates (fresh not dry)
+ Half an aspirin
+ Charms bracelet: a tortoise, a moon, a broken hook
+ Head scarf with neon marijuana leaves
+ Depression on her side of the bed
+ Honeymoon journal converted to recipe book
+ Plastic Ganesh, god of good beginnings
+ Prayer/SOS bell
+ Prescription glasses from 1988 on TV set
+ Silver earring missing its pair
+ *Shhh shh shh*
+ A handkerchief with white lilies, rusty blood
+ Red sauce cooking method on a paper napkin
+ Where winter met spring
+ *I am not going anywhere*

Sleep Tracker

I'm mortified of telling anyone anything
more about Ma in fear I'll run out
of memories like one runs out of one's
favorite pair of shoes, too soon and then
what was once comfort, is now just a bad fit.

Like seeing Ma's face in her sister's
snoring jawline. As if genetics is a joke
god plays to just fuck around with losers:
those that have lost, outstretch palms -

flip Ikea brochures, cover to cover
wonder, how does the little girl (posing
to sleep on memory foam; locked
in the arms of a pretend mom) feel
when the camera's eye is blinking

to capture one perfect shot. To arrest
a breath between takes. To let go
at the call of *action*. I turn my back
to my aunt, look at the sun, start again:

One Mississippi Two

Being a Woman

is to pay rent
to live
in your own body

II.

Apologize

What Spilled Itself Outside the Margin

I am in love with cocktails that taste like cough syrup

I'd marry ginger
if it were willing

Tinder boy who works in climate change cancelled last night.
It was supposed to rain

How do we to sleep and snore
with what we know
about heartbreak and politics and   everything that dies in between?

In my head I look like Deepika Padukone

If not all of her, I can ask the beauty parlor lady to shape
my eyebrows like Deepika's.
In my head I've run
✓   5 miles for 4 days/week, each day marked with a golden*

One Tinder boy got a full-blown anxiety attack
when we were drinking
tea
He'll never get to taste my cough syrup love

To date or not to date.

Masturbation
is becoming more painful than a labored metaphor.

A good vibrator is expensive
as is organic almond butter.
Does abstaining lead to weight loss?

I asked Mr. One Night Stand if I should turn around. You liked me
turned around. Once,
you liked me

I licked One Night Stand's toes like I would have licked almond butter

Sex is a barometer for standard size cool

       To think that ma was admirably pretty and yet monogamous
Say 3 Hail Marys, quick

✓   Must take mom's photo off the wall I face when I masturbate

This is not what mother would have wanted

                  To be this self-aware
to be this foolish

Relationship Status

Humor has a thing for dark spaces
else how can you explain me kissing
my boyfriend hard as the flight blackened
for takeoff, the flight I was taking to go
see my sick mother. I'd find out on landing
that she passed away when my tongue
was busy sampling lust. I reached home
and gargled my mouth with all my lungs
as if guilt can be rinsed & emptied into a sink.
What else is space but a body of dark humor
tied to physical affection like artificial life
support. How else can I explain why I over-
loved every boyfriend after her
with a fondness reserved only for mothers.

Keep Me Burning

I practiced crossing my legs the way my father daggered
his eyes at mother if I wore shorts. Twin openings
exposing more than what they could hold inside.
It took me three sex-ed classes & a crushed pamphlet
to know that I must fold and hold my body like a score
of eggs on a crowded subway. My period premiered
the night we went to watch Godzilla which wasn't as scary
as the sports teacher asking bleeding students to sit separately,
in a lotus pose, a quick whip if the line of our panties showed
through the pinafore. We played telephone with our hands
instead of running in the sun. In Moral Science, the only girl
with waxed legs passed a chit under the smooth wooden desk,
it read *When he touches, I feel hot & cold at the same time.* I lay
naked on our marble floor, fevered. Under his ripped, full-body
poster. I touched myself the way my sister braids and wiggles
her toes, over the phone, under the sheets, coral pink, her words
like submerged seeds on strawberries (who knew those were
achenes, the berry's ovaries). I asked mom what was the big deal
about sexing and she asked me if I'd eaten all my fruit at lunch.
What would Madonna have done? I vibrated all around
my pimpled years with a Walkman or a home karaoke mic
between my thighs knowing there was a sound inside
that would leak on any given Sunday in choir as he'd hit
his solo bits of *Give Me Oil in My Lamp.* If only there was a way
to touch the difference between fill and feel. If only I knew
how I could make origami of my shame and let it fly fly fly.

Tiny Epiphany

Definition: First ever encounter with self

       squirting for 0.75 seconds

Usage: You stop lying to him that you came you came

       you came because you are tired of him

rubbing you the wrong way

Fair Trade

Should make myself a museum of all the come I have helped release. The width between my spread-up thighs is the distance I travel to buy an idea of being loved. Some bodies offer. Some bodies receive. Debit what comes in, credit what goes. The second basic rule of accountancy. The negotiation between giving sex, receiving sex, and enjoying sex. The profile picture of the pursuit of love. A mouth rolled over the full length of a dick, lips blanketing teeth. Thoughts inside head sliding up and down. Your orgasm, mighty boyfriend, is the glue that will bring us together. I count moles on your chest while you're trying to reach your end or wherever it is that the mind goes after a small death. Seven years since mother. My pussy is dry, my mouth is dry. Dripping wet in my appetite for security in labels. Even watching a film is cumbersome with you. Slip on an intellectual condom over the sit back and enjoy part of my brain. I thought my cunt was big & fertile enough a hole to grow stability & commitment from. Stickier it gets, more you feel thirsty. I see your ass getting whipped by your boss in an open plan office. You behind your laptop forecasting peak seasons for glucose powder, slip into my chat window, ask, how do I feel about making us sex only.

Dog: Language: Experts

Bottom-line, you only want to fuck? His face mouths a yes *but chai is allowed.* We drink tea, we fuck, we lunch, we fuck at lunch, he mails me concept cards in five languages, to sell a special nutrition beverage to women with lower.......than others. Assess if the puffery laden copy means the same in intent and action. A word or two could be substituted with tighter emotions. What means strong in Hindi - thick in Marathi, what is resolved in English - ended in Gujarati, I feedback in short hand. He fucks me. Today we are pretending I am the smart one. He post-sex-sighs, *you are talented baby but you need an anchor.* I want to give him some life changing advice too. It's called use your........ on my clit instead. But I need an anchor, friends. Not him, not him. He wants to be an anchor to someone with a husky voice, he's so sure, deep voice is a sign of intellect. Like the 80s actress who only did art films. *Are you sure you won't get attached to me,* he checks so he can rinse out his conscience and his dick after flipping me over, as *doggy baby doggy please* is how we get this job done.

Self-Examination

In the brain I met someone feminist. I took this person to a cafe and read her an Audrey Lorde essay. In the brain I sang the heart's songs about motherhood and teaching my daughter Plath and nights of spooning in bed. In the bed I let the brain undress. I left the brain undressing and in its blue I saw my mother rage, I let Steinem yell at me, I dressed my daughter in full length tights. Despite the summer. Despite the brain. Despite the feminist brain he could push open my thighs or was it his fingers on my waist in passing. In passing through the hallway he spat a slur about my ass having a brain of its own. Was it curvy or firm, rounded or doughy, or fleshy. Does the cushioning of pelvic bone, skin, cheeks and eyes pushed down upon a bed, make a noise? In the brain there is noise and there is someone feminist. In the bed there is silence. There is so much about silence I don't know yet. Does silence like to be spooned? Omitting, revising, humoring are on the guest list to gobble up pain in bite sized portions. In the brain I remember to forget the number of strokes, his hand a hammer, his hand pressing down the back of my head, cerebellum. A structure that coordinates balance. In the brain, a tightrope I make her cross. In the brain I am in control. Do you ever have thoughts of harming yourself, she asks.

To Swim is to Bury An Ocean Inside

i
The neighbor's son was well known
                for backing his car without using rear view
He touched my underwear   I let it slip
I   a minor   between shame and fear   in hindsight
objects in the mirror appear closer than they are

ii
The best therapy is to drink eight glasses of water
every twenty-four hours my mother opened the tap
over my voice. I learnt to drown without being in water

iii
He'd press me
to stay for five more minutes
He'd bait me with two turns at Speed Racer
I'd lie I had probability homework pending
What died of me one evening, stayed afloat as a statistic

iv
so I ran. I ran
A conundrum of conjunctions, my silence: a practiced stage
direction

v
I drank a glass of water. Mother came back to me like the dead
skin falling off my fingers. A student of Home Science,
she had a solution for every stain. If it didn't break down, she'd
suggest
wear a jacket on top, nobody will see it.

Victim Directory

She who went to watch Life of Pi
She who seemed to enjoy it
She who was twenty-two
She who went out to defecate with her sister
She who was asking for it
She who looked like she wanted it
She who wanted to be a photojournalist, lawyer, physiotherapist

,   ,   ,
                            ,   , alive,   ,
, dancing,
She whose mother seemed like a prostitute
She who didn't fight back
She who looked like a ....
She who was the three-year-old of the raped mother
She who was collateral damage
It who was a she-fetus
She who was used to being beaten at home
She who wore a ....
She who was a preemie in pediatrics
She who survived
She who didn't bring us enough Lakshmi
She who was upper caste and yet
She who was an untouchable and yet
She who was an extra mouth to feed
She who loved without permission
She who was born female
She who made it out
She who wrote about it

Self Portrait as First Lines

My thighs are the train's general compartment. Everyone get on board
The uncle who holds my waist like nursing his whisky glass
[You are too attached to yourself]
A woman lives as a woman observing herself from the outside
From the outside it looked like we had a healthy sex life
The day he asked for a video of me pissing
I bought the smaller sized dress to look the part
How are you still so tight?
The jump to zip the fat under my jeans button
Intimacy really gets me off
And the man who gropes my big bum on the bus
And the man who pretends to find his keys near his groin
A knife under my pillow where milk teeth were hidden for wishes
To come true, I wish I hadn't shown him that part of me
Favorite Position: Low self esteem
A girl and her razor walk into a bar
Vitamins, masturbation, and poetry
Love and marriage like clock hands, one chasing another
Brush twice a day
I care if I am kissed
A stand-up comic says to me: You have perfect porn star boobs
How do desire and repression mate?
Always in a trial room, I
A series of reflections, who won't talk to each other

Don't Dip Your Pen in the Office Inkpot

The movie with the 80s actress is the appetizer
served at the beginning of parties that try too hard
to be classy. The question of the lead's sexuality is
left open to. No definite end. Like life. Like death.
Like casual sex. Like my colleague says he will
never let his future daughter have casual sex as he
spoons me after casual sex though I know this
daughter will, we both do, we smoke weed, we
drink tea, we gasp at how Chuck Palahniuk's head
must be so fucked, we fuck, we only fuck. *We*
disappears. Fuck. Fuck. Fuck. Brain throbs at the
speed of sadness. I hear the veins of a leaf getting
crushed underfoot. An arch: the most ticklish gap
in my body: Sex, I have come to you for answers
again All that oh god, oh god, oh godding must
count for something. *So how many men in your books of
accounts,* a male boss quizzes me at my welcome
party. Truth divided by the square root of modesty
plus standard deviation cool is equal to. It took me
years to understand why interest paid is recorded as
an asset, interest received a liability.

Visiting Hours

Sticks and wheelchairs
holding the hands
that once swung me.

Remember: beach day.
Summer on sand
Pa checking the tide,
Ma collecting shells
in her dupatta.
His left hand, her right. Me

in between. Ready for lift-off.
Do it again, I'd scream
Do it again.

Were You Very Close to Your Mother?

If by *very* you mean that my hair is exactly like my mother's,
that I see her shrinking on the pyre every time I see my hair
being defeated by toothcombs, shower floors, stress - then yes.
If by *close* you mean I need to bury the memory of mocking
her for being English illiterate and forgetting to thank her
for single handedly making me not learn, but ace three languages
at school, for teaching me the vocabulary of love without
the crutches of saying I love you, then yes. If by *mother*
you mean that mother will never be just a common noun
on my tongue, that her name even in the utterances of my thoughts
will be the uneven flutter of pages of my favorite book of poems
coming apart. If by *were* you imply my life history being written
on loose leaves in proper cursive, stored in a used carboard file
by my homeopathic family doctor, yes. Give me those sugar pills,
even if placebo, the ones she placed on my tongue every morning
as she braided my hair for school over the lull of grammar revisions:
explain with examples the following: Present Continuous, Past Perfect,
Future Tense.

Won't You Come Give Your Grandmother a Hug?

Why did you yell at ma? Aren't you woman too?
Why did you frown if her rotis weren't perfect circles?
Why did you and her have to wait to eat until the men were finished?
What caused your temper to become soft and formless like old skin?
Why did you have a flip of conscience when she went nuclear?
Does it take cancer to become more compassionate?
Why was your first response to loss, *My son is all alone now*?
How is looking for a new daughter-in-law a form of mourning?
Why was one rejected for her weight? Wasn't she woman too?
Why must you call father's new wife my mother?
Is it because you don't know better?
Should I cut you some slack?
Should I swallow the bones too because you make me the best fish curry?
Should I force my giddy heart to be stone when it sees your vertigo?
Should I look away when you raise your hand
and show me how you wish to dance at my wedding?
Or massage my memories like you, your knee caps?
Discipline me, reject me. Why do you want to hug me?
Am I not woman too?

Poems are Useless

After Amiri Baraka & Jamila Woods

Poems are useless unless they are pepper spray, stinging
cries for change, girls dancing fearless as night. I want
poems my mother couldn't write in her book of recipes.
I want them like golden brown onions sizzling and done
when they are fully translucent, free of color, wishes with
no commas and semicolons holding them back. Every line
a hot skillet of female compromises melting like butter
& scotch. I want a poem for the man whose idea of heaven
is an accidental brush with a woman's side boob. I want it
to be the missing credit of 21 cents for every dollar in her salary
slip. Blemishes my sisters conceal in skin lightening foundation.
Secrets my aunts hide under telephone lines over noise
of television soaps. Each *her* and *her* a particle of raw dust
birthing storms. Every *Her* a dust that cooks, creates, cradles
but never settles.

Bare Facts

The rapist says to the filmmaker:
that 5-year-old girl's life had no value

Tomatoes in the oven
tighten in their skin

You touch my shaven shame & exclaim
It feels like a baby's bottom

My niece in a frock on her first birthday
being changed into boy clothes for a picture

Doctors scurry to white sheet her body
For the story, they give her a new name:

That fake name translates to fearless

Autopsy Reports

Found:

Vagina   knee

soft tissues   intestines   left leg   eye   spine   cervix

uterus   hip bone

flesh   jeans
from thigh   blood   dry blood
                                                            elbow joint

glass bangles   labia   trachea   hymen   rib   dilated anal canal   earlobe

uterus   rib   bra strap   nostril internal   wounds   nailbeds   ankle
                        upper lip   ownership

Last seen:

bruised   ruptured   broken   penetrated   beaten up
        eaten
        cut up
                        cut into   sliced through   sliced into   thrown amidst, thrown
off   rolled of   torn
                        abandoned
                                        left   tied to   hung from   infected by
                                    stamped   gashed
                                    rotting in   rotten

despite   sucked   punched
                                            decomposed
changed   infected by   drowned
                        numbed

                                    strained
            semi-nude   manipulated   fucked
used as   tortured   loved

Dalit Sisters Gang-Raped, Hanged from Mango Tree

Badaun, Uttar Pradesh, 2014

The tree is heavy with confusion
how did it bear fruit off-season?

Circles in the rope perplexed that they overlap
something so tender and so harsh within the same knot.

Villagers in a dizzy drone, directionless like houseflies:
a bobble of heads gathering over anything hot, sweet & edible.

The girls let down one last time by a group of men
for a Two Finger Test. The same two fingers meaning peace

meaning victory, meaning fuck you.

Crime Scene Picture

Badaun, Uttar Pradesh, 2014

Girl[1]   Her sister[2]

hung   hung

from mango

tree[3]

TV CAMERAS[4]

and me[5]

[1] she held tight her insides until it was a safe hour to hunt for a spot to defecate
[2] left home with her source of self-defence, who stood guard
[3] stood breathing, stood still as she was (not in picture: five men)
[4] morphed into pixels, became a shape, in between real estate commercials
[5] viewed by a girl with a remote control. Her hand hovering over the mute button
as she wonders:

is a woman's body a portrait or landscape?

Validation

My body is a brand called validation.
The back of my neck has a bar code
tattooed as a symbol of the product I have become.
From head to toe, toe to head, I have sought validation.
My eyes to begin with - I started wearing contact lenses
because I overheard my grandfather saying...
Who will ever marry her if she wears spectacles?

I move my lower lip over my teeth 50 times – a pro tip
from Cosmo to *rid yourself of that ugly double chin.*
These little breasts have been pushed so high
to stand out, padded to be picked, to be noticed.

So desperate was I to be in the middle of a circle,
that after feeding on a staple Bollywood diet for 21 years
I lay open my senses to names I don't understand,
and still can't correctly pronounce.
Floyd, Scorsese, Goddard, Farhadi,
Nolan, Kundera, Dostoevsky --
The holy trinity of books, films and music
always came along to help me make friends.

I am guilty of holding DSLRs to sunsets
as moments pass me by, of taking countless selfies
to portray myself in the best light.
But this is superficial still, dig deep, so deep
that the need to belong makes me spiral deeper.

And several reluctant blow jobs become proof
that the fear of sleeping alone makes these hands
and this mouth keep a hundred secrets.

That these hips have been suffocating
within drainpipes of denim, sculpting my bottom,
to a most rounded stereotype. I have fit in, fit out,
jumped to fit in, fought to fit in, fit out.

This mad drill, this extensive workout
has reduced me to a mannequin
who sits pretty at a shop window with its monotonous smile,
saying *Pick me pick me pick me.* But it's closing hours now.
And beneath my lensed eyes and dolled up body
is a small voice trying to find its own words.
Let this poem also be validation against validation.

What Do You Have Left in Your Savings Account?

A dead mother. A dead grandmother. Your body shaped like an outstretched
hand, stiff but strong with wanting. Your heart is the square blade at the end
of that oar, the one that must have touched what was left of their bodies.
Your heart is a gentle flutter underwater, invisible at eye-level.
Only in this blueness now can the mothers not be apart. Look, there they are,
both with their cups of chai and TV show cliffhangers, shaking their heads
as you over-salt the dal. Now talking about the weather in your mother tongue,
the one you mark as Proficient on every admission form.

Where do you sign up for a class in entry-level Death? You are tired of speaking
in Gone and After Her. You are tired of believing that they are finding their way
back. As if they are waiting, hunched like old ladies at the door of your mind
with a bunch of wrong keys. Cold metal tapping against a small opening, just
as you are waiting here at the fertility clinic, tapping the back of a green sharpie
on the white space below the question: Why do you want to be a mother?

Visiting Hours

On the last page
of their honeymoon journal,
an incomplete game of Dots –

To play, you must move
by connecting two dots with a line.
When you place the last 'wall'

of a single square, the box
becomes your home.
Believe that a home can be made with lines–

Coda

And if it must enter, let it be called Death
of Disco. Let it be a Wednesday summer,
a ladies' night. The playlist a witness of her past
swinging by, her arms like redwoods, French
kissing the sky, her lips a flute breathing desire.
She will moonwalk in the distance
between the ground and the heel
of a ballerina, uplifted, light like butter
spreading over the body of a knife. Her each step
a clap of a drum competing with off season thunder
and at the call of last orders, she will go hungry
for *one more song just one more* until death
comes asking for one last dance and jives
her to its lonely grave
yard where everything begins to fall
in place. The earth a baseline for opening
eyes of the curious mind. She and her death, arms
locked, will trace the silver earring missing,
the mother's untimely leaving, the father
cussing, the heavenly filling, that other
worldly feeling when she leans in to hug
endings. On her surface marigolds
will breathe and the sky like celebrating
Holi will be painted in twenty-one colors
of the sun setting. By next evening, she
and dying will become one pure flame
of whisky going down throats
with no mouths
open for goodbyes.

ENDNOTES

❖ In "Unremember", the line *What could I have said to raise you from the dead* is taken from Sufjan Stevens' song, Fourth of July

❖ In "Stopgap" the term "item song girl" refers to item girl, an urban Indian slang for promiscuous woman. In Bollywood, women who dance in (provocative) item songs are called item song girls.

❖ *Saat Samundar Paar Main Tere Peeche Peeche Aa Gayi* is a song from the film, Vishwatma (1992)

❖ Every Twenty Minutes a girl is raped in India. Source: National Crime Records Bureau

❖ "Dalit Sisters Gang-Raped, Hanged from Mango Tree" and "Crime Scene Picture" are based on a true incident: PTI Report by The Times of India, May 28, 2014

ACKNOWLEDGEMENTS

I am grateful for my mother and all the ways she taught me love. Papa, thank you for your trust in me and for lessons in inscrutable strength. To Ravikant, who realized I was a writer before I fully knew myself to be one.

To all the women who are my sisters and my friends, and those whose stories I wish to tell. This book would not have been possible without your courage, thank you for inspiring me and speaking to my silences.

My deepest thanks to my first poetry teacher at University of San Francisco, Doug Powell. Thank you so much for your generous feedback and for pushing me to be better. Your faith in my ambition and my voice fuels my desire to make more art. Thank you, Bruce Snider for your guidance and the effort you took in reading every single draft. Rachel Richardson, I am immensely grateful to you for helping me shape this book and for blessing my several anxieties with your resounding confidence. Barbara Jane Reyes - I am better because of your writing, thank you. A big thank you to all my classmates at University of San Francisco, especially Alan Chazaro and Shelby Dale Deweese for being invested in my work and helping me through every line.

Thank you to my biggest cheerleaders, Rochelle D'silva, Shubhodeep Pal, A.F. Mathew, Amelia Willoughby, Vinita Agrawal and Menka Shivdasani. To Linda Ashok at RædLeaf Foundation for Poetry & Allied Arts, thank you for your vision and your commitment to poetry that is relevant to the world that we live in. And to Robert Archambeau (Judge, *RL Poetry Award 2017)* for understanding the spirit of the manuscript.

Finally, many thanks to the editors of the following journals in which some of these poems, in some version have appeared:

Anti Heroin Chic: *Self Portrait as First Lines*
Airplane Poetry Movement: *Validation*
Boaat: *Relationship Status*
Boston Accent Lit: *Don't Dip Your Pen in the Office, Inkpot, Fair Trade, Shorthand: Violence*
Francis House & Best Indian Poetry 2018: *Water Logging*
HEArt Journal: *Crime Scene Picture*
Juked: *Poems are Useless*
Noble Gas Qtrly: *Last Rites, Self-Examination*
Packingtown Review: *Repair & Maintenance*
pif Magazine: *Genealogy*
Lines+Stars: *Unremember*
The Bombay Review: *The Science of loss*
The Knicknackery: *Saat Samundar Paar Main Tere Peeche Peeche Aa Gayi, i am thirteen and a half years old*
Threepenny Review: *Admission*
VAYAVYA: *To Swim is to Bury an Ocean Inside*

Other winning titles published by
RLFPA EDITIONS include

Best Indian Poetry 2018

RL Poetry Award 2017

Editor's Choice: Betel Nut City by *Shalim Hussain (India)*
Teaching Father how to Impregnate Women by *Soonest Nathaniel (Nigeria)*
Mother Tongue Apologize by ***Preeti Vangani (India)***

RL Poetry Award 2016

Somewhere but not here by *Stephen Byrne (Ireland)*
Apostrophe by *Barnali Ray Shukla (India)*
Editor's Choice: The Land below Water by *Manik Sharma (India)*